# TRAVELLING AROUND
# MONTALBANO'S PLACES

Dan Stark

*"South-eastern Sicily is culture at its best expressions"*

M. Fuksas

# INDEX OF PLACES

# INTRODUCTION

The great success of the TV series "The Inspector Montalbano", from the very first episode (The Snack Thief, 1999), brought hitherto little-known scenarios before the eyes of many people, stimulating great curiosity right from the start.

Reproducing what is narrated in a book on film requires great meticulousness and care, because it is very difficult to find natural locations that almost perfectly mirror those narrated in novels. But it is precisely here, according to many, that the secret of success lies, namely in the choice of the province of Ragusa as the setting for the adventures of Italy's most famous inspector. The Hyblaean province, with its Baroque scenery and unique natural landscape, starting from the Hyblaean heights and winding its way through typical dry stone walls and a few masserias, until it reaches the sea embanked by beautiful golden beaches, offering a scenario perfectly parallel to that described by Camilleri in his novels.

These undisputed elements played a decisive role in enabling the drama to achieve its success, which can be summed up in the unique beauty of the locations that provided the backdrop.

Through a wide-ranging landscape review rich in history, culture and traditions, it is hoped to stimulate curiosity and the desire to visit this particular corner of Sicily, one of the few that still manages to preserve an old-world charm, and which, not by chance, possesses works and places that have been declared UNESCO World Heritage Sites.

# DONNAFUGATA CASTLE

We want to start this journey from one of the oldest and most fascinating places in the province of Ragusa, the Donnafugata Castle.
On the set, the castle depicts the villa of the mafia leader Balduccio Sinagra and the estate of Baron Piscopo of San Militello.
The episodes "The Trip to Tindari - Montalbano's Arancini - Par condicio - The sand track" were filmed here.

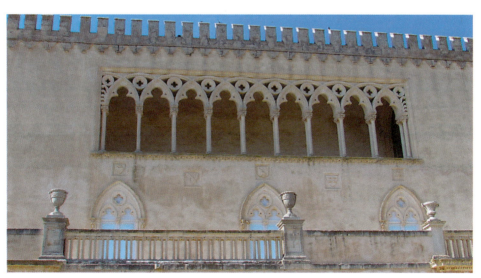

*Details of the Castle*

*The Castle...* A late 19th-century aristocratic residence of the wealthy Arezzo De Spuches family, it covers an area of approximately 2,500 square metres and has a large neo-Gothic façade, crowned by two lateral towers. The construction was made with typical Ragusa stone, which was divided into three parts: the soft part was used to build the façades, statues and all the mouldable parts; the hard part was used for the structure and flooring; the middle part was used for everything else. In addition, the so-called black stone (stone with pitch) was used in some rooms to give the floors a special polished effect.

The castle, divided into three floors, has more than 120 rooms, about 20 of which are still accessible to visitors today.

Each room is decorated in a different style. Worth visiting are the music room with trompe-l'oeil paintings (paintings with an 'eye-catching' effect), the great hall of coats of arms of all the Sicilian noble families (a room that is used for various ceremonies), the hall of mirrors and the so-called bishop's flat, with splendid Boulle furniture.

Over the years, the castle has also been the location for several film and television sets in addition to Inspector Montalbano's. In fact, some scenes from the film I Viceré and many scenes from Luchino Visconti's film Il Gattopardo were filmed in the "billiard room".

Surrounding the castle is a large and monumental 8-hectare park with more than 1,500 plant species and various "distractions" designed to delight and entertain guests, such as the circular temple, the Coffee House, some artificial caves with fake stalactites and the peculiar stone labyrinth.

*The particular entrance of the labyrinth*

*An overview of the labyrinth*

# PUNTA SECCA

We continue our journey by visiting the famous home of Inspector Montalbano. The latter is located in Punta Secca, a small hamlet in the municipality of Santa Croce Camerina, a place that in the fiction is represented as "Marinella", the ancient fishing village where the inspector lives.

*Above the house and below Punta Secca seen from the lighthouse*

*In both photos the Inspector's home,*
*above seen from the sea and below from the beach*

Inspector Salvo Montalbano's home on the fictitious beach of Marinella was once used as a warehouse.
Today, however, the house is a Bed and Breakfast.

*The house as it once was*

*A series of photos and views of the house from various angles*

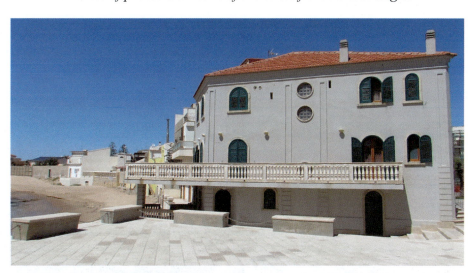

Just opposite Montalbano's house stands the ancient *Scalambri Tower*, which in the past served as a watchtower against probable raids by Saracen pirates. Continuing our visit to Punta Secca, not far from the tower, we find the house that in the fiction is presented as the home of Pino Catalano (see image page 17), in the episode "The Shape of Water".

Walking towards the seafront, we reach Faro Square (see image), where various evening entertainment shows take place in the summertime.

*Amerigo Vespucci seafront*

Also on *Faro Square* stands the majestic 35-metre-high LIGHTHOUSE, which every night since its construction in 1853 has never ceased to perform its signalling function.

Almost at the end of the Amerigo Vespucci promenade we find the "Enzo a Mare" restaurant, where the Inspector goes from time to time, alone or in company, for lunch or dinner.
Some scenes in the episodes "The Paper Moon - The Sphinx's Wings - August Heat - Angelica's Smile - A Night Voice" were filmed here.

*A sunset seen from the restaurant*

# HISTORICAL OVERVIEW

Punta Secca, like the whole of Sicily, has been influenced by the various dominations that have succeeded one another on the island over the centuries, but from the earliest times it has always been a strategic junction in the great chessboard of the Mediterranean sea.

The name Punta Secca derives from an outcrop of rocks in front of the eastern beach, creating what is known to the locals as a sea shallow (secca).

In antiquity, Punta Secca was part of a larger territory called "Le Kaukane", given its proximity (about 1 km) to the Byzantine anchorage of Kaukana, an important landing place of the Byzantine Empire from the 4th to the 9th century AD.

Later, during the 9th century AD. Punta Secca was occupied by the Arabs, who gave it the name "Ra's Karama", from which today's "Capo Scaramia or Scalambri" derives, as it is indicated on some nautical maps.

From the early Middle Ages, however, following the Norman invasion in 1061, it too came under their rule a few years later.

Then in 1140, the small fief of Santa Croce Camerina, including Punta Secca, was donated to the Abbey of St. Mary la Latina of Jerusalem, under the administration of Filippo d'Argirò (Agira).

During the 16th century, in order to ward off pirate and Arab incursions, an armed watchtower was built by the Bellomo family of Syracuse to defend the landing place, and two warehouses (one is currently the fictitious home of Inspector Montalbano, while the other is Palazzo Arezzi) flanked by the tower were built for the use of the landing place.

The tower was part of a ship sighting system and was in contact with the tower of Mezzo (or Pietro tower) 2 km further north, with the Vigliena tower of Punta Braccetto, 4.2 km also north of Punta Secca, and with the Cabrera tower of Mazzarelli(Marina di Ragusa) located 5.5 km to the east.

In spite of everything, Punta Secca has always remained sparsely inhabited, and it was only after the construction of the lighthouse (in 1853) by architect Nicolò Diliberto Danna that it began to be populated.

Towards the end of the 19th century, in fact, the rich bourgeoisie of Santa Croce Camerina obtained from the Princes Trigoria di Sant'Elia (heirs of the Marquis Celestri) the first building plots and permits to build holiday homes. This trend, after having suffered a setback during the two world wars, started to develop again from the 1950s onwards, giving the hamlet its current configuration.

# MARINA DI RAGUSA

Continuing along the coast after Punta Secca, we arrive at Marina di Ragusa, another small town overlooking the sea.

*Carmela Panebianco's home in the episode "Cat and Goldfinch"*

*Angela Biondolillo's home*

*Tower Square - Livia Boccadasse's Home*

Starting from Angela Biondolillo's home, one can walk along the Mediterranean promenade until reaching Tower Square.

The latter has been refurbished to allow the Mediterranean seafront to join the Andrea Doria seafront.

For several years now, Marina di Ragusa has been awarded the title of Blue Flag, a special recognition awarded by the FEE (Foundation for Environmental Education) to all those seaside resorts that meet certain environmental quality criteria.

There are also two restaurants on the Andrea Doria seafront: Il Delfino and Trattoria da Carmelo (see image above). Some scenes from the episode "The Sand Track" were filmed in the latter.

*A glimpse of the beach as seen from the Andrea Doria seafront.*
*Some scenes from the episode "The Paper Moon" were filmed here.*

# HISTORICAL OVERVIEW

Marina di Ragusa only assumed its current name in 1928, but in fact its original name was "Mazzarelli".

The latter derives, according to the most widespread opinion, from the Arabic word "Marsa"(port) which in Italian in plural diminutive becomes Mazzarelli (small ports).

In fact, the area (inhabited since the Upper Palaeolithic era) has over the centuries been an important trading point for the various successive peoples. The first to benefit from its location were the Greeks, who, after naming the local river "Irminio" in honour of the Greek deity Hermes, established a port at its mouth, thus fostering the development of a large commercial emporium. The area, like the rest of the territory, saw the succession of various dominations, from the Roman (212 B.C.-535 A.D.) to the Byzantine (4th-9th century A.D.), from the Arab (9th-11th century A.D.) to the Norman (from 1061 until 1296).

Following the Sicilian Vespers of 1296, the Aragonese took over, with whom the County of Modica was born, but Mazzarelli would only become part of it in 1392 with the settlement of Count Bernardo Cabrera.

Thus began the long period of the Cabrera family who, under Ludovico II, built the watchtower against the Saracen invasions between 1585 and 1596, favouring the development of commercial activities in the area in front of the tower, and exactly opposite the current customs square or "scaru viecciu" (old port) as it was called by the locals.

Between the end of the 17th century and during the 18th century, the commercial activity of exporting agricultural products from the interior increased, particularly with traders from Trapani, so much so that the point where they docked was named "Scalo Trapanese" (Trapanese port).

The relocation of the trading post caused the tower to fall into disuse, so that between 1884 and 1886 Baron Paolo La Rocca Impellizzeri pulled it down to build the palace that still stands today. All that remained of the tower was the terrace.

At the end of the 19th century, however, a new trade took hold, that of pitch, which gave the port a further boost.

But from 1920 onwards, this trade also began to decline, giving way to fishing and agriculture.

Since the post-war period, however, fishing has increasingly given way to tourism, so much so that Marina di Ragusa, with its new marina built in 2009, is now one of the most fashionable holiday resorts in south-eastern Sicily.

# DONNALUCATA

Continuing along the coast, after Punta Secca and Marina di Ragusa, we find Donnalucata and then Sampieri. In the episodes "Artist's Touch" and "The Voice of the Violin" one of the houses on the seafront in Via Marina is the house of Anna Tropeano.

# SAMPIERI

In the coastal area of *Pisciotto*, in Sampieri (a hamlet of Scicli), we then come across the ancient *Fornace Penna* with its peculiar arched structure. It has been a habitué of many episodes of the Inspector. Many scenes in "The Shape of Water - The Sense of Touch - The Smell of the Night - The Sand Track - The Three-Cards Game - The Spider's Patience" were filmed here.

*Fornace Penna (La Mànnara)*

# SCICLI

We now leave the coast and begin to climb towards the Hyblean mountains. The first town we reach is Scicli. We start our walk from Piazza Busacca (see image), here we notice Palazzo Busacca (bottom left) where the Questore's press conferences are held. Between the Palace and the Church, we can see the bed of the St. Mary La Nova stream. This is where "The Treasure Hunt" and "The Voice of the Violin" were filmed.

We now move to one of Scicli's most important streets, Via Francesco Mormino Penna, which has been declared a UNESCO World Heritage Site in its entirety.

The first building that stands out is the Town Hall, which in the fiction depicts the Vigàta Inspectorate. Just think that this building is seen in no less than 14 episodes, amidst the comings and goings of police cars and walks of various kinds.

Walking down the aforementioned street we can admire the other monuments. Descending to the right we notice a peculiar Pharmacy (featured in the episode "The Smell of the Night") and Spadaro Palace (featured in the episode "The Sphinx's Wings").

All in an astonishing mixture of Baroque and Rococò.

*(On the following pages a series of photos)*

*Town Hall*

*A stretch of street Francesco Mormino Penna*

## La Farmacia (Pharmacy)

## Spadaro Palace

Let us turn back now. We move towards Piazza Italia, where we pass two important palaces: Penna Palace and Fava Palace (featured in some episodes). Continuing along the road between the two palaces we reach the Church of St. Bartholomew, featured in the episodes "Par Condicio - Cat and Goldfinch".

*Penna Palace*

*Fava Palace*

*Some details of Fava Palace*

*Church of St. Bartholomew*

Opposite the aforementioned church is the contrived house of the Todaro Family, present in the last two episodes mentioned above.

Finally, from Piazza Italia, looking up from below, one can see The Convent of the Cross, where several scenes from the episode "The Potter's Field" were filmed.

# HISTORICAL OVERVIEW

Scicli's name is thought to derive from Siclis, a name used in antiquity to refer to the Siculians, the famous people of the sea whom the Egyptians called Sheklesh.

The city extends over a wide plain set within three narrow valleys known as Quarries (the valley of Modica, the St. Mary La Nova quarry and the St. Bartholomew quarry, where the church of the same name still stands today), which originated from remote tectonic fractures and over time became the bed of torrential streams.

It should be noted, however, that the ancient city stood on the St. Matthew hill, where the Convent of the Cross and the remains of a castle still stand today, making the ancient settlement difficult to conquer.

Human presence in the Scicli area dates back as far as the Eneolithic period, i.e. between the Copper Age and the Early Bronze Age

(3rd-2nd millennium B.C. - 18th-15th centuries B.C.), as evidenced by the findings in the Maggiore's cave and various other caves in the area.

Like the rest of the territory, Scicli too saw a succession of different dominations over time, from the Greeks to the Carthaginians and then to the Romans (during which it became a "decumana" city, i.e. a city subject to a tribute consisting of the payment of a tenth part of the harvest).

The Romans were succeeded by the Byzantines, but it was only under Arab rule during the first half of the 12th century that Scicli experienced a period of flourishing agricultural and commercial development never before experienced.

In March 1091, however, following the battle that took place in the Piana dei Milici, Scicli was definitively liberated from Saracen rule by Count Roger of Altavilla and passed to Norman rule.

Also linked to this battle, which took place in the Plain of the Milici, is the legend of the Madonna of the Milizie. In fact, it is said that the final battle was won by the Christians through the intercession of the Virgin Mary who descended on a white horse to defend the city. The small church of the Madonna of the Milici was later built on the site of the event and the battle is commemorated every year with the Feast of the Milizie, one of Scicli's main folkloric attractions.

The Normans ruled from 1091 to 1195 and made Scicli a state town, introducing the feudal system already widespread elsewhere.

The Normans were succeeded by the Hohenstaufen, and when the latter fell in 1266, the Angevins took over. However, the exploitative policy of Charles I of Anjou was the cause of an insurrection known throughout Sicily as the Sicilian Vespers (Vespri Siciliani). Thus, in April 1282, Scicli together with Modica and Ragusa rose up against the local French garrisons and placed themselves under the protection of Peter III of Aragon. During Aragonese domination, the city then became part of the County of Modica, following its fortunes under the Mosca (1283-1296), Chiaramonte (1296-1392), Cabrera (1392-1477) and Enriquez-Cabrera (1477-1742) families.

The population, which had increased considerably over the years, unfortunately suffered a drastic reduction of almost two thirds following the plague of 1626 and the terrible earthquake of 1693. But from this rubble Scicli managed to be reborn in a new architectural style, the Baroque, enriching itself with those 18th-century buildings that still adorn the town today.

# ISPICA

From Scicli, continuing eastwards (first on the SP75 and then on State Road 115), we arrive in the easternmost town of the province, Ispica.

*St. Mary Major Square*

As soon as we arrive, we take XX Settembre street and head straight towards the city centre, making our first stop at St. Mary Major Square, where we can admire the Basilica of St. Mary Major with its distinctive Loggiato (see photo), which appears in the episode "The Paper Moon". For the design of the Loggiato, which delimits the square, architect Vincenzo Sinatra was directly inspired by Bernini's colonnade in St. Peter's Square.

Continuing along XX Settembre street, we arrive at Unità d'Italia Square, where we can admire Bruno Palace and the mother church of St. Bartholomew.

*Unità d'Italia Square with Bruno Palace to the right*

*Church of St. Bartholomew*

Moving to the north side of the church of St. Bartholomew, we can walk along Garibaldi street, where various scenes in the episodes "The Sand Track" and "The Sphinx's Wings" were filmed inside some 19th century buildings.

Also appearing in the same episodes is the Church of the Holy Annunciation, which is located at the end of Garibaldi street right on the square of the same name.

*Church of the Holy Annunciation*

Both the square and the entire church were filmed in the episode "The Sphinx's Wings".

# HISTORICAL OVERVIEW

Ispica, as a human settlement, is the oldest municipality in the province of Ragusa. Its origins, as evidenced by the ancient caves still present in the Ispica Quarry, date back to the time of the Siculians (15th-7th centuries B.C.).

However, the town was formerly known by the name Spaccaforno, which it retained until 1935. The name of the town has always been uncertain in nature. According to some, it derives from the Greek phrase "gupsike kaminos" (hot furnace), which would therefore explain the name Spaccaforno; according to others, it derives from the name of the river Hypsa, which once flowed through the valley and which would explain the name Ispica. But among the many versions, the most credited is that of a corruption of the Latin locution Hyspicaefundus (bottom of Ispica Quarry), a name it had during Roman domination.

Like the neighbouring towns, Ispica too has seen the alternation of different peoples over the centuries, from the Siculians to the Greeks, from the Romans to the Byzantines, from the Arabs to the Normans, and many traces of their passage can still be seen today inside the Ispica Quarries. However, it was the Arabs (9th-11th centuries AD) who built the first settlement.

After the Swabian and Angevin domination, in the 14th century, the alternating historical events of the town began, which ended up in the possession of the viceroy Berengario di Monte Rubro (Monterosso), treasurer of the kingdom, who upon his death gave it to Queen Eleanor of Anjou, wife of King Frederick III.

Peter II, King of the Kingdom of Sicily, then granted it as a fief to his brother William, Duke of Athens, and from him it passed to his butler Manfredi Lancia. After being confiscated from the latter's heirs, the city was granted as a fief to Francesco Perfoglio in 1375. After following the fortunes of the county of Modica, it passed to Andrea Chiaramonte, until 1392, when by the new King of Sicily Martin I, Spaccaforno and the entire county of Modica were ceded to Bernardo Cabrera. It was later detached from the County of Modica in 1453 when it came under the rule of Antonio Caruso from Noto.

In 1493, it was then brought as dowry by the latter's daughter, Isabella Caruso, to her husband Francesco II Statella, whose heirs maintained it until the abolition of feudalism in the 19th century. Here too, however, on 11 January 1693, the terrible earthquake that struck the whole of Sicily manifested itself in all its violence, razing the entire town to the ground. The latter, most of which had previously been located inside the Ispica Quarry, was later rebuilt in the flat area outside the quarry.

Some neighbourhoods were rebuilt around the churches that remained standing, while others sprang up ex novo, but despite this, the ancient settlement was never completely abandoned (it is used every year during the Christmas period for the performance of the living nativity scene, which is highly recommended).

Eventually, however, the intense and lengthy period of reconstruction led to the birth of the architectural beauties that still characterise the city today, some in Baroque style such as the churches of St. Mary Major, St. Bartholomew and Holy Annunciation, others in Art Nouveau style such as Bruno Palace and Belmonte Bruno Palace.

# CAVA D'ISPICA

Not too far from Ispica, we penetrate into the Modican territory, reaching the ancient caves of Cava d'Ispica. Here we will find ourselves in front of a real prehistoric city with thousands of natural and artificial caves that will take us back through the centuries.

*"The Gymnasium", above seen from the outside and below from the inside*

Among the countless caves, the one that has been filmed is the "Larderia Catacomb", where in the episode "The Spider's Patience" Montalbano finds the bag full of counterfeit money left for Susanna Mistretta's ransom.

*Larderia Catacomb*

# MODICA

Continuing up the province we arrive at Modica

*Panoramic views of the town of Modica Bassa*

The city of Modica is divided into two parts: Modica Alta and Modica Bassa.

The latter is rich in monuments and is characterised by the presence among the historic houses of peculiar narrow streets and stairways all interconnected almost as if to form a labyrinth (one of these is Maggiore Barone street, in the episode "The Sphinx's Wings"). Modica, known as the city of a hundred churches, has also been recognised by Unesco as a World Heritage Site.

*St. Peter's Cathedral*

*St. Peter's Cathedral (other angle and details)*

At the top of the quarry, behind the cathedral, the city clock can be glimpsed. The cathedral's majestic late Baroque façade surmounts a wide staircase with straight ramps, punctuated by the presence of statues of the twelve apostles, represented in high relief.

The main artery of Modica Bassa is Umberto I Avenue, full of fascinating monuments on both sides. One of these is an ex Jesuit Convent, now the Palace of Public Education, which in the TV series in question represents the Vigata prosecutor's office.

Moving on now to Modica Alta, we mention the home of Nicolò Zito, the "Tele Libera" journalist featured in many episodes of the series, including "The Trip to Tindari". Continuing along this road we soon arrive at St. George's Cathedral (pages 54-55). To the left of the cathedral, Polara Palace can be seen.

*The House of Nicolò Zito*

*Typical coat of arms*

*Polara Palace*

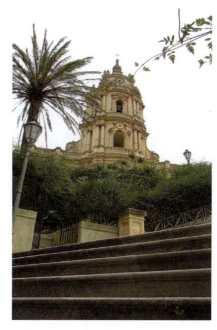

Climbing the adjacent steps to the right of the cathedral, we reach Guerrazzi alley. In this alley some scenes were filmed in the episode "The Sand Track".

*In both photos Guerrazzi Alley*

Behind the cathedral there is Moncada street.
Some scenes in the episode "August Heat" were filmed here.

*Above Moncada Street uphill.*
*On the right Moncada Street going*
*down intersecting with Polara Street*

# HISTORICAL OVERVIEW

According to legend, the birth of Modica is attributed to the heroic God Hercules. In order to honour the help he received from a beautiful Greek woman in finding the oxen that had been stolen from him (Hercules' tenth effort), he founded three cities on Sicilian soil and gave one of them the name Motia.

Actually, on the basis of studies conducted in the area, it is believed that the city was inhabited since the Eneolithic period (3200-2200 B.C.) and that it was founded by the Siculians around 1360 B.C., giving it the name Mùrika. In fact, the name Modica derives from Mùrika, which means bare rock. With the arrival of the Greeks in Sicily in 756 B.C., the Sicilian populations of the coast were forced to flee more and more to inland towns, including Modica, but before long they all came under Greek control.

After the Greeks it was the turn of the Romans, who after having conquered Syracuse occupied Modica around 213 B.C., giving it the name Mothyca and turning it into a decuman city (Roman colony). The Romans were followed by the Byzantines, who exerted a profound influence from a religious point of view by erecting numerous churches. But the city, which was highly developed commercially, was attractive to many.

Thus it was that the Arabs, in 844-845 A.D., after a short siege, conquered the city and ruled it until the arrival of the Normans in 1090. Norman rule gave way to Swabian rule in 1194, which was then succeeded by the Angevins in 1270. Like the other towns in the province, Modica rebelled against the Angevins' bad policies, culminating in the uprising known as the Sicilian Vespers in 1282. It was then that the Modicans drove out the French and appointed Federico Mosca, leader of the uprising, governor of the city.

After the proclamation of Frederick II of Aragon as King of Sicily, by virtue of the concession diploma given by the latter to Manfredi di Chiaramonte as Count of Modica, on 25 March 1296 the County of Modica was born as an autonomous multi-feudal entity.

For about 500 years, the county became the richest and most powerful feudal state in Sicily and southern Italy. The investiture as Count of Modica automatically coincided with that of Viceroy of the Kingdom. And the Chiaramonte family had that privilege, ruling the County until the death sentence of the last Count, Andrea (guilty of plotting against the crown), in 1392. This sentence, according to chronicles, was engineered by Bernardo

Cabrera, a Catalan condottiere instrumental in the conquest of the Kingdom of Sicily. By getting rid of the last heir of the Chiaramonte family, he was given the go-ahead to be named Count of Modica, as a sort of reward for his services to the crown.

Subsequently, in 1481, when Bernardo's niece, Countess Anna Cabrera, married Don Federico Enriquez, cousin of Ferdinand the Catholic, the County passed into the hands of the Enriquez-Cabrera family. Under this dynasty, the County experienced a long and prosperous period, interrupted only by the earthquake of 1693.

Post-earthquake reconstruction, however, was rapid and eventually saw an even more beautiful Modica, because it was reborn in its monuments in full Baroque style. Just eleven years after the earthquake, all the churches in the city were accessible. But the early 1700s also marked the end of the Enriquez-Cabrera family, following the revocation of the investiture of Giovanni Tommaso, on charges of treason.

The County of Modica was then included in the Spanish demanio, and then came into the possession, between Italian (Victor Amadeus II of Savoy) and Austrian (Charles IV) brackets, of the Bourbon dynasty, who reigned until the advent of the Unification of Italy.

Following the latter event, in 1861, Modica became a district capital, and remained so until 1926, when it lost its supremacy following the appointment of Ragusa as provincial capital. The city, however, despite being administratively downsized, has continued to develop economically over the years in agriculture, animal husbandry and handicrafts.

Moreover, after being included in the list of World Heritage Sites by UNESCO in 2002, it has also experienced a remarkable tourist development, linked to the unique beauty of its Baroque monuments and its famous chocolate.

# RAGUSA

Leaving Modica behind and continuing along State Road 115, we arrive in the provincial capital, Ragusa.

The latter is divided into Ragusa (the new part) and Ragusa Ibla (the old part). Entering the town from the SP25 we continue straight on Giuseppe di Vittorio

avenue and Archimede avenue. After almost two kilometres, we leave Archimede avenue and turn right onto Giosuè Carducci avenue. We follow the latter all the way to the end and then turn right onto Fante avenue. From here on, we continue straight ahead and after reaching Liberty square we pass it, continuing along Dr Filippo Pennavaria avenue, until we turn left near Traspontino avenue. And here we are at our first stop, the old

Capuchin Bridge (see photos on page 60), filmed in the episode "The Snack Thief".

After seeing the bridge, we turn back onto Pennavaria avenue. We then continue downhill until we turn left onto Giovanni Meli avenue. We continue straight ahead on the latter and cross the Pope John XXIII bridge. After about half a kilometre we cross Corso Italia avenue (Ragusa's main artery). We take it, turning left to go up it, until we reach St John Square.

In the centre of the square we can admire the Cathedral of St. John the Baptist, where the Curia premises were used to set Arturo Pecorini's butcher's shop in the episode "The Potter's Field".

*St. John the Baptist Cathedral*

*Premises of the Ragusa Curia*

*Bishop's Palace*

After paying our attention to the Cathedral and the nearby Bishop's palace, we can continue our tour by walking down Corso Italia avenue. After a few hundred metres we arrive in Matteotti square, where the Post Office palace stands out from view. The building, both internally and externally, was filmed in the episode "The Trip to Tindari".

*Post Office Palace*

We continue down Corso Italia until we reach house number 73, adjacent to Bertini palace. We find ourselves in front of an almost abandoned palace, the subject of the opening scene in the episode "The Treasure Hunt".

This is where Montalbano finds the first clues in what will turn out to be a long and tortuous search, full of enigmas and continuous puzzles, without knowing, however, that what is at stake, in this case, is his own life.

*Detail of Bertini Palace*

We now continue on Corso Italia avenue, descending until the road narrows. It is here that our journey into the ancient Ragusa begins, namely Ragusa Ibla.

# RAGUSA IBLA

Ragusa Ibla is most probably the most representative city of the imaginary Vigata, on the one hand because it is the location where most of the scenes in the various episodes were filmed, and on the other because it is the baroque city par excellence in the province (declared a Unesco World Heritage Site). Arriving at the end of Corso Italia avenue, we descend the steps of the stairs that take the place of the street on the right. We immediately come across the *Church of St. Mary of the Stairs*, from where we can admire a fascinating panorama of Ibla, in all its extension. The church, together with its adjacent maze of stairs, have been featured in many episodes of the Inspector, including: "Montalbano's Arancini - The Treasure Hunt - The Paper Moon - Cat and Goldfinch - The Sphinx's Wings - The Catalanotti Method".

*Church of St. Mary of the Stairs*

Continuing down the steps of the various stairways, or alternatively along the winding road, one arrives at a fork in the road, near which is the imposing Cosentini palace. The latter, although not featured in the fiction, has some Baroque details that are definitely worth admiring.

*Cosentini Palace*

*Hyblean Gardens*

From this point on, we walk along Market Street, embarking on our journey on foot through the endless alleys of Ibla. After reaching Giovan Battista

Odierna square, we enter the greenery of its enchanting gardens, captured in some of the scenes in the episodes: "The Seagull's Dance - The Paper Moon - A Diary from '43 ". Once outside, after a short, relaxing walk, on the left, about ten metres away, you can admire the ancient St George's Portal.

*The main avenue of the Gardens and the famous St. George's Portal*

*Municipal Delegation Building at Pola Square*

*Church of St. Joseph*

Walking along XXV Aprile avenue, after passing the Church of St. Thomas, we find on the left the Trattoria La Rusticana, which in the fiction is the famous Osteria Don Calogero, the Inspector's favourite haunt (in the first episodes) for refreshments. Continuing on, we arrive at Pola square, where we find the Municipal delegation building and the nearby Church of St. Joseph. These places have been filmed in many episodes: "The Turning Point - The Shape of Water - The Voice of the Violin - The Sphinx's Wings - The Spider's Patience - The Three-Cards Game - August Heat - The Paper Moon".

Coming up from Pola square, on the left we find Del Convento alley (see photo on the right), a peculiar little street where a scene in the episode "Par Condicio" was filmed. Instead, always starting from Pola square, turning right we walk along Orfanotrofio street. Along this way we find Di Quattro Palace (see photo below). Further along, still on the same street, near broad Camarina, we come across Battaglia Palace. Both palaces were filmed in the episode "The Paper Moon".

Immediately after passing Battaglia Palace, we notice Count Cabrera street on the left, which leads us onto Duomo square. Scenes from the episodes "The Snack Thief - The Voice of the Violin - The Shape of Water - The Three-Cards Game - The Seagull's Dance" were filmed on this street.

*Battaglia Palace*

*Count Cabrera Street*

*Count Cabrera Street seen from Duomo Square*

*Duomo Square seen from Count Cabrera Street*

Another building featured in the Inspector Montalbano fiction is the *Circolo di Conversazione* (dating back to the fascist era). In the following photo Duomo Square seen from the Circolo di Conversazione.

Finally, from the square, one cannot fail to notice the famous St. George's Cathedral, the most spectacular religious building in the entire province. Work on its construction began in 1744, while those of the peculiar railing in 1889.

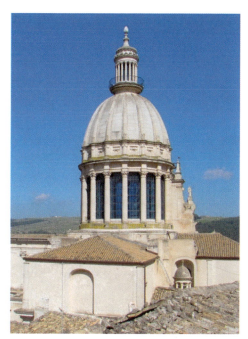

*A close-up view of the cathedral dome*

Returning in the footsteps of our Inspector, we should also mention Capitano Bocchieri street, just behind the cathedral. Here we can admire in all its baroque splendour *La Rocca dei Sant'Ippolito Palace*, the site of some of the filming in the episodes "Montalbano's Arancini - Par Condicio".

*La Rocca dei Sant'Ippolito Palace*

# HISTORICAL OVERVIEW

The name Ragusa derives from the accusative plural rogous (rogus) of rogus V, a term that in Sicily and Magna Graecia indicated the granary, i.e. the grain places.

The origins of Ragusa most likely date back to the early Sicilian period. According to studies of the area, it appears to be the heir to Hybla Heraia (named after the goddess Hera, protector of the fields), an aggregate of Sicilian villages that stood near present-day Ragusa Ibla. It came into contact with Greek and Roman populations and reached a certain importance in the Byzantine period (700 A.D.), when the city was provided with a castle.

However, its reputation for grain production attracted the attention of the Arabs, leading them to conquer the city in 848 AD.

The latter kept it under their rule until the advent of the Normans in 1091. Norman rule then saw the transfer of Ragusa, as a fiefdom, from Count Roger to his descendants, until the Swabians took over in 1194. The Swabians were followed by the Angevins, but the latter were driven out following the notorious Sicilian Vespers revolts of 1282. The city thus passed into the hands of the state.

After the birth of the County of Modica in 1296, Ragusa became a fief of the Counts Chiaramonte, following the fate of the County also under the Cabrera and Enriquez-Cabrera families.

The city remained the administrative seat of the county until 1447, when, following a popular revolt by the people of Ragusa against feudal abuses, Giovanni Bernardo Cabrera transferred the administration to Modica. But the episode that marked a turning point in the city's history occurred in 1452. From that year on, thanks to the first concessions of the right of emphyteusis, a new category of bourgeois landowners was slowly fostered.

The wealthiest among them, through the acquisition of noble titles, gave rise to a new minor nobility with a certain strength. In fact, the introduction of emphyteusis initiated a real economic revolution, slowly delineating the new agrarian landscape, characterised by a dense network of muri a secco (dry-stone walls), built to enclose the new properties, to divide the fields used for grazing and to allow the rotation of cereal and leguminous crops.

However, this led to a new struggle between the new and the old nobles. Both, in order to increase their prestige as much as possible, subsidised the construction of new churches for this purpose, also acquiring the right of patronage (ius patronatus) over the chapels adjacent to their palaces (with the encouragement and blessing of the clergy, who gained in revenue). It was during these years that the first parochial struggles were witnessed, between the inhabitants of the parish of St. John, known as "Sangiovannari", and those of the parish of St. George, known as "Sangiorgiari".

These struggles were perpetrated for centuries, both before and after the terrible earthquake of 11 January 1693, when many of the towns in south-eastern Sicily, including Ragusa, were destroyed. In the aftermath of the earthquake, when it came to deciding on the reconstruction of the city, many of the parties disagreed.

Unable to reach an agreement, in the end most of the old nobility preferred to rebuild it where it had stood before, while the massari and the new bourgeoisie preferred to build the new buildings in contrada Patro, thus favouring the birth of the first nucleus of Ragusa Nuova, characterised by wide, straight streets.

This led to the birth of two Ragusas: Ragusa Nuova or more simply Ragusa, and Ragusa Vecchia or Ragusa Ibla. Both, despite the fact that many people considered this to be an absurdity, remained characterised by separate administrative lives for many years, until they were reunited into the current provincial capital on 6 December 1926.

Despite the fact that socialist ideas circulated in the early 20th century, Ragusa was named the first city of the fascist empire in Sicily. It was bombed throughout World War II, until the Allied landings in 1945.

The end of the war, hailed with joy, also brought with it unprecedented economic growth, primarily in industry and agriculture, which together with the ancient beauty of its monuments (declared a UNESCO World Heritage Site) continue to mark Ragusa as a dynamic and prosperous city.

# "MASSERIE" IN THE PROVINCE OF RAGUSA

We now leave Ragusa behind and head towards Comiso. Along the way, we can see the characteristic Ragusan Masserie (farmhouses), which together with the typical muri a secco (dry-stone walls) and carob trees dot the countryside of the province.

The term *Masseria* indicates a farm (agricultural holding) characterised by a large fortified rural building. It includes not only the owner's lodgings but also those of the farmers, the stables, and the stores for fodder and crops. The *Masseria* in itself re-proposes the scheme of the house with an agricultural courtyard in the Mediterranean tradition (a single large central space - court or courtyard - also serving as a threshing-floor, overlooked by the entrances to the various residence and work buildings, known in Sicilian as "U Bagghiu"). With the latter it almost always has in common the enclosure, consisting of a high, fortified wall.

# COMISO

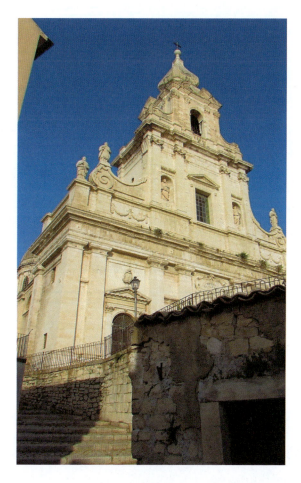

Here we are in Comiso, also known as "Stone Town". Among the monuments worth visiting are: the 19th-century Town Hall in Municipal Square, the 17th-century Iacono-Ciarcià palace, the Castle of the Counts Naselli d'Aragona, the Church of St. Francis, and the mausoleum of Baldassarre III Naselli. Also noteworthy is the 16th-century Church of the Annunziata, the former Byzantine Temple of St. Nicholas. But let us return to the footsteps of our Commissioner. We head for n. 16 of San Biagio street, to admire the Church of St. Mary of the Stars and the nearby Herbs Square. Some scenes in the episode "Montalbano's Arancini" were immortalised here.

*Dome of the Church St. Mary of the Stars*

*Herbs Square*

*Diana Fountain Square*

*Castle of the Counts Naselli d'Aragona*

# HISTORICAL OVERVIEW

The first traces of human settlement in the hilly area of Comiso date back to the Neolithic and Eneolithic periods. In this area, the Siculians established flint workshops, which were mined, worked and exported.

The name of today's town is thought to derive from ancient Casmene, a Syracusan sub-colony of the Greeks located at Cozzo di Apollo, a hill in the Hyblean mountains immediately above Comiso.

Like the rest of today's Ragusa territory, after the Greek domination Comiso also experienced Roman domination, during which it was called Jhomisus, and later Byzantine domination, when it took the name Comicio, in honour of their birthplace Comizo. Byzantine rule (4th-9th centuries A.D.) brought a slow but steady growth of the town, which later progressed under the Arabs (9th-11th centuries A.D.), with the construction of the first muri a secco (dry-stone walls) that still characterise the surrounding landscape today. However, the foundations of the future town were laid when the Aragonesi, settled in 1296, ceded Comiso to a certain Federico Speciario of Messina, who had a palace-castle and other fortifications built in the urban core.

From 1321 onwards, the fiefdom underwent several cessions, from Berengaro De Lubera to Giovanni Chiaramonte, and from the latter to the Riggios, before passing to the Catalan Bernardo Cabrera in 1392, thus becoming part of the County of Modica.

But the real turning point did not occur until 1453, when, due to a serious economic crisis, Giovanni Cabrera, Bernardo's son, ceded Comiso to the Naselli, nobles of an ancient family who held control of the fief until 1816, achieving exceptional economic and social results. The latter, thanks to modern laws appropriate to the new times, such as the granting of estates in emphyteusis, the establishment of free fairs, the granting of franchises and various other measures, succeeded in giving the city a period of splendour never known before. The only dark interlude that slowed down these processes of renewal occurred in the 17th century, during which there was a notable demographic decline in the population, following the foundation of the nearby town of Vittoria in 1607, the terrible plague of 1624 and the tragic earthquake of 1693, which caused deaths and enormous damage to the town. However, the people of Comiso were able to rise again from these ugly events, and thanks to the climate of building fervour of those years, new public and private buildings, churches and other monuments were built in the characteristic Sicilian Baroque style that is still visible in its distinctive features today. In order to revive the city from the sad events of the past and give it a new economic impetus, the first industrial factories were set up in Comiso thanks to the benevolence of the Naselli family, such as the paper mill built in 1729 and the soap factories built in 1742. These, however, were the last years of splendour for the Naselli family, which from then on began its phase of decline, culminating in 1816 with the suppression of feudality in Sicily. This opened the door to strong social renewal in Comiso too, first under the Bourbons and later under the Kingdom of Italy. This period of reform slowed down considerably with the advent of the First and Second World Wars. The only positive note of those years was the construction of an airport. The latter, initially used for military purposes, was only in recent years (and after many political battles) inaugurated as a civil airport, thus allowing for an airfield in the province of Ragusa as well. From the post-war period onwards, in addition to a discrete growth in the agricultural sector, the city of Comiso, thanks to the presence in its territory of a limestone in many respects similar to marble, started a form of stone-processing industry that is still highly developed today, and that has given it the appellation "Stone Town".

# VITTORIA

Not far from Comiso we arrive in the town of Vittoria, the youngest municipality in the province. Places to visit include: People's Square, Town Hall (Iacono Palace), Carlo Alberto street, Church of St. Joseph, the Old Industrial Building, the Municipal Theatre. Returning to our route, however, we pause at a few points in particular, including *Ferdinando Ricca Square*, where St. John's Cathedral stands (see photo).

Scenes in the episodes "The Three-Cards Game - The Sense of Touch - The Terracotta Dog - The Spider's Patience - Angelica's Smile" were filmed in the said square. Opposite the Cathedral we find Calatafimi street. Coming down from here, just a few meters later, we notice Colonna Square. In the latter square some frames were filmed in "The Spider's Patience".

*Dome of St. John's Cathedral*          *Cathedral detail*

*Colonna Square*

*Interiors of St. John's Cathedral*

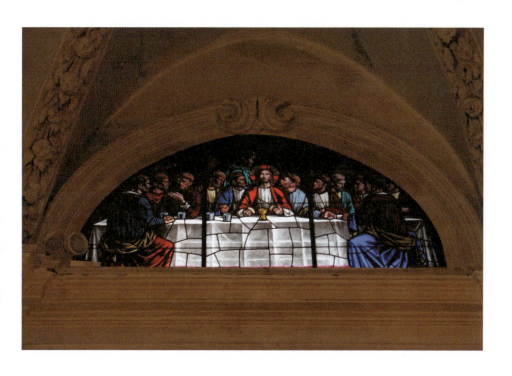

## People's Square and Municipal Theatre

## Garì Fountain

# HISTORICAL OVERVIEW

Vittoria is the youngest municipality in the Hyblean province, its foundation dating back to only 1607. However, the present area was already partially inhabited since the Bronze Age, as evidenced by clear archaeological remains from the Imperial Age (2nd century AD) and the Byzantine era (early 9th century AD).

The town owes its name to its founder, Countess Vittoria Colonna, wife of Count Luigi III Enriquez-Cabrera of Modica. Upon the latter's death in 1599, the countess, unable to derive any benefit from the fiefs in Spain heavily exploited by her husband, turned her attention to the County of Modica to increase her family's economic and political influence in the area. After having identified, on the instructions of the county governor Paolo La Restia, a vast and luxuriant plain in the area where ancient Kamarina was located, in the territory of Boscopiano (today known as the "Grotte Alte"), he decided to lay the foundations for the building of a new town.

After obtaining royal authorisation, the countess, in order to encourage the growth and populating of the new town, granted all settlers who went to live there privileges, franchises and exemption from taxes for the first few years.

This immediately favoured a rapid development of the town, which over time took on its current urbanistic appearance, characterised by a chessboard layout, where the modern is mixed with Art Nouveau buildings and Neoclassical and Baroque monuments.

Unlike the other towns in the area, the 1693 earthquake did not cause much damage here, and therefore the pure Baroque reconstruction that the other neighbouring towns underwent did not occur.

Vittoria does not possess very old monuments, but several Art Nouveau palaces deserve attention, including: Pavia palace, Trama palace and Piazzese palace. Over the years, the expansion of the town also involved the small fishing village of Scoglitti, originally used as an import and export dock and inhabited mainly by fishermen.

The economic activity of the town, which for many years in the past was mainly linked to the cultivation of vines and the production and trade of table grapes, received a great boost with the development of greenhouse vegetable cultivation after the middle of the 20th century, as evidenced by the presence of one of the largest fruit and vegetable markets in Italy.

*Aerial view of Punta Secca (1980s)*

# to do list

# food

relaxing

# experience

# shopping

Printed in Great Britain
by Amazon

44751152R00059